Ground

Anna Milbourne
Illustrated by
Serena Riglietti

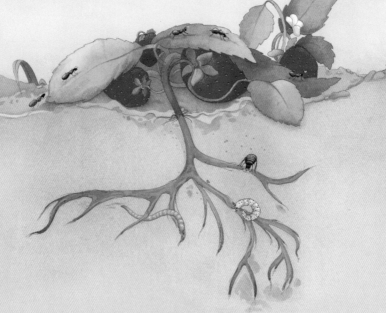

Reading consultant: Alison Kelly
Roehampton University

This story is about

Lenny

and Lola

and what they find
under the ground.

"What's under the ground?" asks Lenny.

First they find
plant roots

and an ants'
nest.

A mole is eating
a worm.

slurp slurp

8

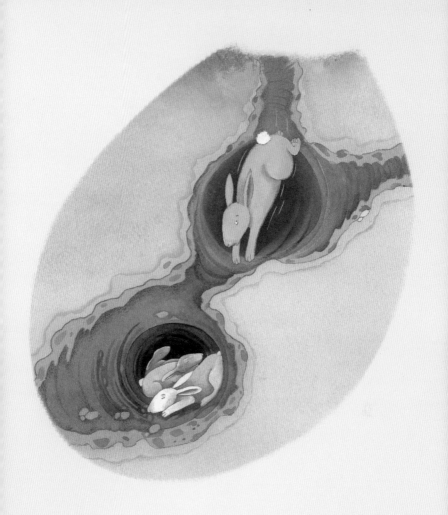

Rabbits snuggle
in their burrow.

Lenny and Lola dig deep under their house.

There are lots
of pipes.

There's a rumble
in the tunnels.

12

Trains zoom by.

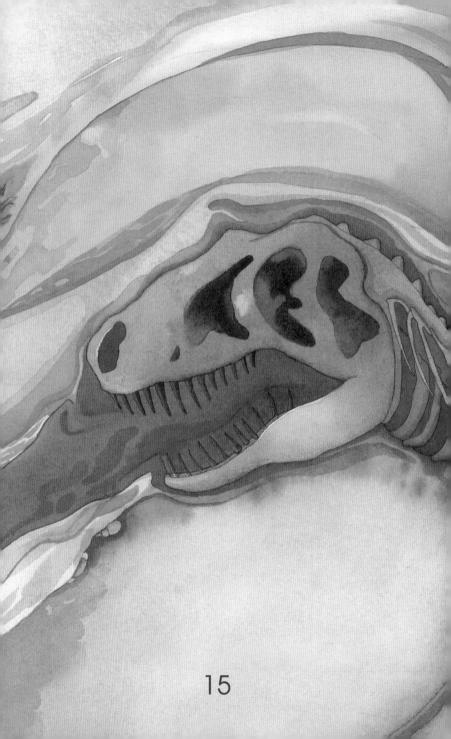

They discover
a damp, dark cave.

Now they are
in a mine.

Lola and Lenny
dig deeper.

19

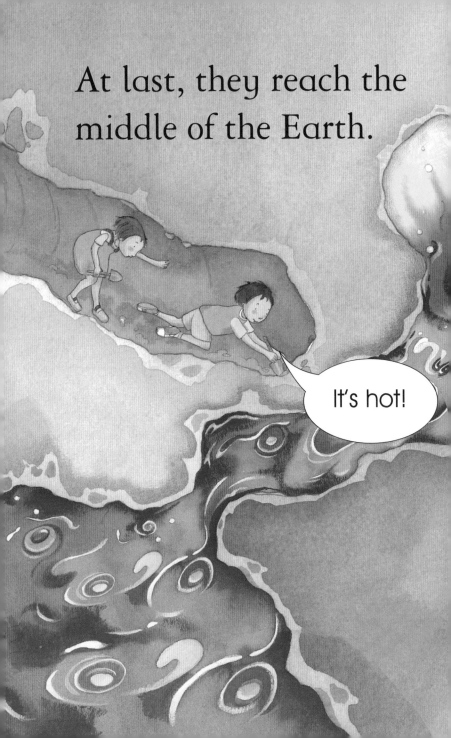

They dig...

and dig, until...

...they pop out on the other side of the world!

About the Earth

The Earth is a big, round ball. Here it is cut in half so you can see inside:

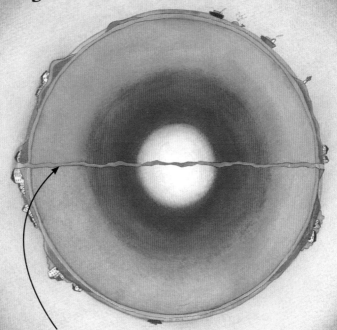

This is where Lenny and Lola dug.

PUZZLES

Puzzle 1

Can you match the animals
to their homes?

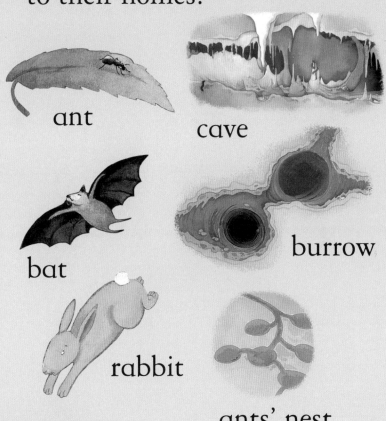

ant

cave

bat

burrow

rabbit

ants' nest

Puzzle 2

Can you choose the right
speech bubble for each
picture?

Puzzle 3

Can you spot the differences between these two pictures?

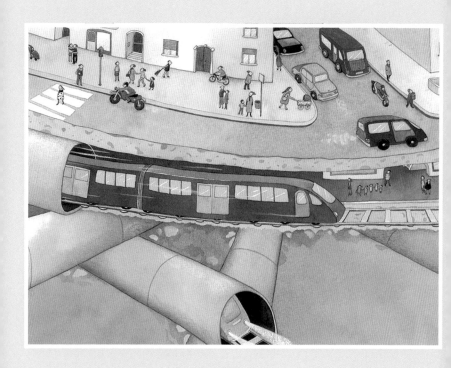

There are six to find.

Answers to puzzles

Puzzle 1

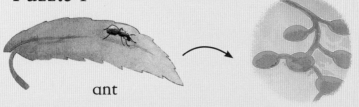

ant

ants'
nest

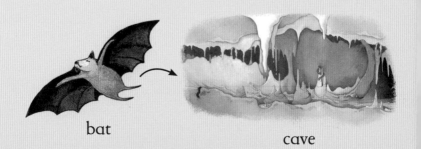

bat

cave

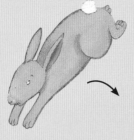

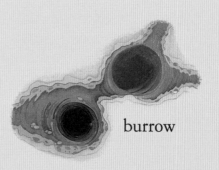

burrow

rabbit

Puzzle 2

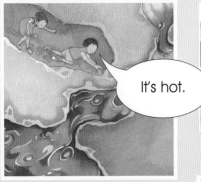

Puzzle 3

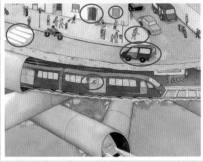

Consultants: Professor Dorrik A. V. Stow
and Drs. Margaret and John Rostron
Design: Emily Bornoff
Series editor: Lesley Sims
Digital manipulation: Nick Wakeford

This edition first published in 2011 by Usborne Publishing Ltd.,
Usborne House, 83-85 Saffron Hill, London EC1N 8RT, England.
www.usborne.com
Copyright © 2011, 2006 Usborne Publishing Ltd.